THE FRENCH COLLECTION

DANIEL SIMON PIERRE

Dr. Daniel Simon Pierre
The French Collection

Published by BooxAi
ISBN: 978-965-578-647-7

PREFACE

"The French Collection Vol. #1: A New Beginning" is a compilation of new poems and a selection of non-Christian poems from my first three books. It aims to connect with a diverse range of readers and followers, offering a glimpse into my original thoughts, ideas, feelings, and private emotions. Throughout this book, I share personal experiences, both joyous and challenging, from both my public and private life.

I'd like to express my gratitude to my wife, Yolene, for being a constant source of inspiration, even though much of my writing reflects my experiences as both a young, single man and a married man.

I give thanks to my daughter Sarah Daniella for financing this book project.

I believe that readers will find a strong emotional connection within these pages, identifying with the parallelism expressed in the poems and discovering reflections of their own lives. My advice to readers is to immerse themselves fully in the experience: find a comfortable spot, perhaps with a glass of Merlot or Chardonnay in hand, elevate their feet, and dive into the world of my poetry. Dim the lights, set the mood with classical music or soft rock in the background, and let the words take you on a journey.

My intention is straightforward: to keep it authentic, to awaken dormant emotions—whether they be good or challenging—and to encourage readers to reflect on their past, present, and future.

Above all, I aspire to connect with each reader on a personal, emotional, spiritual, psychological, and physical level. This book is just the beginning; more new poems and books will soon be in print, reaching out to a wider audience of readers and supporters.

Dr. Daniel Simon Pierre

IN MEMORIAM

Where are they now great men and women of the past?
That paved the way for us all

From Toussaint Louverture and Jean-Jacques Dessalines,
who set us free from the shackles of tyranny and slavery?

To those of old who built the great pyramids and
formulated the Pythagorean Theory,
from various descendants of mighty kings and great
queens and royalty of majesty
to the queen of Sheba, the most beautiful queen of
the East
from the kingdom of Axum in Ethiopia?

From the great Mahatma Gandhi, also known as
'Ganghiji' and 'Bapu'
who suffered much pain, humiliation, and tyranny in his
own country, and fasted for
freedom and equality for his people and country?

To the humble and passionate and non-violent civil rights
leader Dr. Martin Luther King,
who paid dearly with his life, and was martyred for the
cause of justice and equality?

From Rosa Park, Edger Everett, and all the martyred sons
and daughters,
who demanded respect, fairness, and equality, and refused
to give up their seats?

To the admirable Nelson 'Khulu' Mandela,
who ultimately paid a great price and sacrificed his life for
more than 25 years?

And now finally to Barak Hussein Obama,
who knew that he could accomplish the long-foretold
dream and make it a reality:
'Yes, we can'

RASTAFARI

Rasta
Rasta man
Rasta man vibration positive

Bob
Bob Marley
Bob Marley and the Wailers
Jah Rastafari

Haile
Haile Selassie
Haile Selassie Emperor of Ethiopia and Prophet of the
Rastafarians
Jah Rastafari

Ziggy
Ziggy Marley
Ziggy Marley and the Melody Makers
Jah Rastafari

Dread
Dreadlocks
Dreadlocks naturally groomed and uncut
Jah Rastafari

Roots
Ganja

Splits smokes by all true Rastafarians
Jah Rastafari

Claat
Bloodclaat
Bumboclaat
Raasclaat
Jah Rastafari

Reggae
Reggae music
Roots, rock, reggae, this is reggae music
Jah Rastafari

Fried dumplings, ackee, and cod fish
Jerk chicken, pork, and fish
Oxtail, curry goat, fish escovitch, brown stew chicken run
down, pepper pot soup
Plum juice, Irish mush, and sorrel juice
Jah Rastafari

I SHALL RISE

Risen from the pages of deceptions, despair, and
disappointments.
I shake up the dust of the past,
lifted my head above the clouds,
and gaze at the more hopeful and promising horizon

Indeed, I am alone,
the worst has passed and vanished away in thin air,
and the best is yet to come

A new beginning is ushering at dawn,
for distant and unpleasant memories are gone

I will rise to a new beginning,
to a new chapter without ending,
where life and the future will be sweeter,
forgetting of the past that made me so bitter

Risen from the nightmares of my life,
to my destiny and what God has in store for me,
I shall rise

Risen from the depth of poverty and my sad reality,
to fulfillment and victory,
I shall rise

A seed or two of hope were implanted deep in me,

yet, I found myself alone and lonely to raise them,
I shall rise

A bitter separation, a nasty divorce, or being a widow,
cannot hold me back, because yet I shall rise,
I shall rise

And even when I was rejected and misused,
mentally, physically, and/or emotionally abused,
I shall rise

I shall rise
I shall rise
I shall rise

THE SCORPION LOVER

She pierced my tender heart with her sharp torn,
poison my vulnerable senses with seductive venom,
the love portion she alone uses to captivate her prey

Entrapped in the snare of her love,
I found myself weak in her presence,
losing all control, reason, and good judgment

I can't, I can't resist her powerful aura,
the aroma of sensuality overwhelmed my inner being,
privately and convincingly saying to myself, I want more

Intoxicated by her charm and trait,
my knees buckled under the weight of her love before I hit
the floor,
not really understanding what just got over me

My only desire now is to become her prey,
for her to do as she will, oh have mercy on me
wish me well, for I don't know what to expect

This long-legged-femenine of a woman,
gentle, charming, enchanting.
Wow! I wonder how it would be?

She secures me firmly in her gentle arms,
embracing me with such passion and seduction,

caressing me endlessly before

Finally kissing me with such tenderness,
my tongue intertwined with her in a labyrinth of love,
warm, fuzzy, and juicy it feels

Losing control and no real desire to stop,
as a gush of oxygenated warm blood flows to my head,
I melted in her arms like dark rich chocolate

Tears of joy running down my cheeks,
not bashful of the way I fell now or what the outcome
may be,
wishing that this ecstatic joy that I'm experiencing would
last for eternity

She moved, dinned me, and grooved me,
to the sound and rhythm of a sweet melody,
watching and making each calculating moves with
meticulous perfection,
surely summer as come, for I surely feel quite warm and
wet deep inside

OASIS OF LOVE

The desert of my life is dry, arid, and parch

Sad and lonely nights have been constant in my life
passing and hanging over my head like an immense black
cloud of despair.
Trees naked without limbs, branches, or even leaves,
no shades or covering

Desolation, depravity, and the sad reality
but just when I thought dying of thirst was the only
solution
you came into my life and brought me hope and joy
The joy to live and survive the condition of my state mine
I found that oasis of love in you

Rounded shape of comfort makes me feel secure
dark rich soil for the new grass to grow and the royal palm
trees roots to anker
Now finally, and finally now the sparrows have a place
to rest
fresh cool water to base my thirst,
enough for the camels to drink before departing for their
long journey
smooth and smooth bolder serving as a sanctuary

TIME

What is time? Even where is it? When shall we find it?
Is it just a mere figment of our vivid imagination?
Or an endless continuum of infinite movement
Is it purely seconds carefully adjusted by the expensive
Timex?
Maybe consecutive minutes kept watchfully by the
timekeeper
Perhaps unaccounted hours lost in space each day seeking
to make amends
From a to z, from zero to infinity, found in the black hole
or continuum of life
In the twilight of space or the twilight of the night. Or the
twilight zone of time
And just like sands in an hourglass, times keep dripping
away one at a time
Do we have enough of it? Even if we should? Then what
would we do?
Wave of ambiguous moments passing away, but precious
time remains constant
The continuum of life in fact never ceases but flows
through time
For it is indeed profound, baffling, and dubious
Time is of the essence, the essence of life itself
For in the beginning it was, and in the end, it will be
For indeed there is a beginning and surely an end
The end of his world, or the end of time itself
Alone time is self-sufficient and endless

Reliable and never late, that is the time!
As written in the good book, time is destining and
appointed
A time for every wish and season
A time for every rhyme and reason
So, I ask, do you have the time?

FIELD NEGROS

Strong, rugged, uneducated, brute, and unpolished
Brash, wild, untainted, and unwilling to obey
Ruff on the edges, muscularly hard
Always trying to run away on each occasion
Not wanting to be shackled, domesticated, and controlled
by the master's chains
Rusted, tight to the ankle's bones
Cutting to the marrow and oozing precious ancestral
blood
The blood of their forefathers flows deep within
Inside all the veins of their foremothers
Coming from the first over shipman of precious cargo
Stacked high as packaged sardines for eminent delivery
To a land far away with no return address or an inquiry

HOUSE NEGROS

Refine, polish, and fair silky skin
Combed, straight, greasy, and partially curly brown hair
Educated, can spell, and read some easy lines
Controlled, calm, and behaves properly
Like sheep, docile, example and demonstration of proper
mannerism
Yes, Sir, she answered politely with her head looking
down at the stoned floor
Her masters' often called for choirs and fetched some
errands nearby
To do all perfectly and meticulously before sundown
Belly distended by month's end, soon to reveal the
identity
Light fair-skinned, straight hair, grey eyes baby, seed fruit
from the master's one prowling predatory night.
She was defenseless, couldn't say no, not truly free,
you know
For she is regarded, just like the rest, as possessions
belonging to the plantation
Just like cattle or live stocks, priced daily to determine
their value

HERALD

Who is he, that good news who came into the world?
To save it from its perversion and destruction

To save the sins of all for all
So that all humanity can find salvation

Salvation found only in him through the shedding of his
precious blood
To purge, purify, save, and sanctify

To forgive, forget with no regret
That all man can and won't forget

The sacrifice of the lamb of God carried on Golgotha
Slayed on the rugged cross shamefully

Bleed to purify all humanity
And all those who believe in his name

Who is this bearded lamenting Jew?
His name is Jesus Christ of Nazareth

THE THRONE ROOM

Ushering the holly of hollies
There he sat on the throne of grace
Behold the perfect lamb of God which took away the sins
of the world

So majestic, incorruptible, and shinning with holiness
The son of God, the Son of man, the Savior, the Messiah,
the lion of the tribe of
Judah, the lineage of David, the Christ, Jesus himself

Standing before him the twenty-four elders in worship and
adoration
To his right flank the cherubim with their two edges
flaming swords
To his left flank the Serafin, with two winds covering their
feet, two wings
Covering their faces, and two wings hovering in his
presence
The righteous, the saints, the saved, those who accepted
him as their Lord and
personal savior and trusted in his message of salvation,
and those that tarry and
who kept the faith?

Were prostrate before his feet, saying repeatedly in
unison; Holly, Holly, and Holly
is the Lamb of God, who is sitting on the throne?

FALL FROM GRACE

Here we are, men and women of so-called integrity,
Here we are, standing on the throne of grace.
In the presence of all mighty God

Spiritual hypocrites we are, God doesn't know us
We wear our blue suits and white dresses thinking we are
holly,
Like old decrepit roaches going on a shopping spree
of sins

Spiritual hypocrites we are, God never knew us

Shopping for sins and pleasure, that is,
Directed by lust, greed, and our inept inability to resist
temptation and the desires of the
Flesh

Spiritual hypocrites we are, dogs depart from me,
says God

Steadfast in the word of our merciful God the father
For God, he temps no one, for he can't be tempted

Spiritual hypocrites we are, our names are not written in
the Lamb book of life

On Sundays, we come to church well-groomed as if we

were going to be wed;
And on Mondays, we commit adultery with the church
secretary or our neighbor's wife,
Hastily preparing our funeral

On Sundays, we mount the pew of salvation as though it
were our private business;
And on Tuesday we steal, rob the poor, and the weak
among us

On Sundays, we shoot praises and thanksgiving with our
holly lips;
And on Wednesdays, we curse and call our brothers and
sisters 'Raca'

On Sundays, we give God our offerings, tidings, and gifts
as good sacrifices;
And on Thursdays, we sell drugs to our fellow men

On Sundays, we clap our hands in joy and render a
handshake;
And on Fridays, we beat and abuse our wives and children
with those same hands

On Sundays, we preach an inspired apostolic message of
salvation and redemption;
And on Saturdays, we break every rule, ordinance, law,
and commandment ever written

Fall from grace, spiritual hypocrisy

POVERTY WAS A DISGRACE

Poverty was my name and I was ashamed,
poverty was my name, but I wasn't the one to blame

I was born in the ghetto of Harlem,
a place that I regretted being from

Son of an illiterate and alcoholic father,
son of a whorish and irresponsible teenage mother

There I was poor as I am,
who can free me I asked with pity

My father was a sanitation worker with his bottle by his
side,
my mother was pregnant and had me at thirteen

I was born in poverty!

Their mediocre income was not enough to support us,
but they gave birth to four plus,
Shironda, Shemiqua, Sheniqua, and Latisha

A cloud of poverty and despair hung over our heads,
Nothing to eat but some dry stale bread

My father came home always drunk, dirty, and smelly,

My mother couldn't care for herself, dropped out, barefooted

On welfare, receiving food stamps, government handouts, and handdowns,
I guess my sisters were destined to follow in her footsteps;
Ugly, unable to control their raging hormones, babies having babies

I was born in poverty!

There I was, looking like a skeleton,
Unable to support my own weight,
My stomach touched my spine, dry bones uncovered by flesh showing

Poverty smelled terrible!

I smelled like an old, humid piece of damp dirty rag,
My clothes were disheveled, and torn up

They were worn out, patched up, full of unwanted holes and missing bottoms,
Many nights I slept on the cold and dirty floor
Hungry, frightened, unable to shed a tear,
I was too weak to speak, too weak to scream;
Sometimes I fainted when I could no longer take it

I knew poverty!

We didn't own a damn thing,
We were too poor to afford anything

The only thing we had coming,
Food stamps, Medicaid, and welfare checks on the first of
the mount

The mailman was our best friend,
Only he could truly understand

But when he was late,
He became our worst public enemy;
We dared him to call in sick or even think of missing
his date

I knew poverty!

We live in the project housing in Manhattan,
A large ghetto city of no man's land

Our one-bedroom shack,
Was the worst in this stinking place

It looked like an abandoned crack house,
A shelter for abandoned, stray, and lost animals

Broken windows, old led paint peeling off the cracked
walls,
The cold hardwood floor had enormous gaps

Serving as a sanctuary for the uninvited fat rats,
Infested with huge flying reaches, spider nests, and
prehistoric flies

I hated poverty!

My neighborhood was filthy, polluted with slimy worms
and carcasses of dead
Domesticated animals,
Oh! God, why me?

Trash piles and overflowing dumpsters line the sidewalks,
Poodles of water ran the deserted streets,
Mosquito lava erupted from the damp mud,
The residents were distraught, disfigured, discouraged,
and lethargic
Feeling sorry for themselves, careless, shameless, and
blameful of others,
There is no way out

Crime, prostitution, theft, vandalism, drug use, and
unemployment were at their peak;
We didn't own anything; everything belonged to the slave
masters, the white man

I hated poverty!

I walked miles to school on an empty stomach,
Tired, sweaty, dusty feet

Use clothing, faded, and wrinkled,
Smelling like mildew and roaches' nests

Purchased from the thrift shop,
Given by the Salvation Army

Kids glared, laughed, and taunted me,
I didn't have any friends, poverty was my only companion

I was lonely, rejected, and impoverished,
My lunch was a dry peanut butter sandwich

God save me from my misery!
What I have done to this world?
I often asked myself

What I have done to this world?
For many nights I wasn't fed

Was it the color of my skin?
Was I paying for my sin?

God, save me from my misery,
Life for me had no meaning;
A terrible, horrible, and humble beginning

When I opened my eyes, poverty surrounded me,
When I tried to breathe, poverty penetrated me,
Thus, I talked, looked, and behaved as a poor child

Poverty was a disgrace!

What the future holds for me?
What must I do to be free?
Only God can deliver me,

Only God can give me a dream

For poverty for me was a disgrace

THE ENEMY WITHIN

Who are you Mr. and Mrs. AIDS?
What are you?
Who conceived you?

Why are you so evil, destructive, and deadly?
Where do you belong? In hell perhaps!

What are you?
What made you?
Tell me, my enemy, how do you look?
You are an odious disease,
Destructive and devastating you are, oh AIDS!

Why do you treat me as such?
You infiltrated my body and made me weak
You traveled my bloodstream and infested me
You ate my substance

My bones are cancerous and fragile
My flesh is rotten
My skin is dry, flaky, and lumpy with painful sores
Fouls odor overwhelm my surface
You stole my hair for your canopy
In me you seek your refuge, why?

I'm young, but my frame feels old

I'm young, but my body is weak
What must I do? But to wait!
Wait, for my fallen peak

CONGRATULATION

Roses are red,
And violets are blue

You love him,
And we are certain he loves you too

May the good Lord truly bless you both,
As you grow in spirit and truth

May the everlasting and unconditional love of God mix
with your love and keep you both
joined forever

Again, congratulations on this exciting day,
and may God richly and gracefully bless you both

GOD AND US

Two hearts, one love
Two tastes, one choice
Two ideas, one will
Two persons, one life
Two kids, one family
Two mistakes, one sin
Two sins, one forgiveness
Two destinies, one destination
Two deaths, one life
Two roads, one heaven
Two wrong decisions, one eternal burning hell
One Savior, one joyful eternal life
Thank you, God, for loving us
Thank you, Jesus, for saving us
Thank you for choosing us to dwell in paradise with thee

MOTHERLAND

Vast fields of lush dense greenery carpet the land
As the wild beast, lions, and giraffe runs freely

Villages of haft naked and haft dressed nomads not
ashamed,
To see the real, them as they were created

Paid and purchased safari for pure amusement and for the
kill,
Like the thrill of killing, in the rush of satisfaction

Hunts and shacks line the hillside, the ravines, and basins,
With echoes of joy or laughter resounding from the
mountaintop

Lions, king of the jungle, predators and carnivores kill
to eat,
Unlike the white men and uncaring foreigners who kill
for joy,
assessment, and trophies

HAITI: PEARL OF THE ANTILLES

Haiti is the precious first black free negro slave nation of
the Antilles
Shinning bright like the biggest star far away in the
firmament
High above the Milky Way eliminating the constellations

Majestic royal tall palm trees line the sidewalk of Chant
De Mars
For the midday casual strollers and merchants to find
sanctuary from the scorching
rays of the sun or for the hard-working women merchants
enjoying the last money exchange
moment and of a brief siesta

Gorgeous white sand beaches, look like bright crystal
But smooth and soft under the soles of the American and
European tourists
Cabanas covered with dry old plantain leaves
Serving Five Star Barbancoo Rum on ice, soothing
cremas, and refreshing cool
Coconut water, which has just fallen from the porch partly
unrouted tree

Majestic iron and metal cruise ships from all over the
world line the ducks like infantry
soldiers marching for battle

Or as the indigenous Tainos entering their hunts after a
successful hunt
Happy multiple ethnics, mostly Caucasians from the U.S.
debarking from
enjoying themselves, purchasing low priced artifacts from
the country artisans

Quabosal and The Iron Market busting with business and
exchange of currencies from the tourists
Deals and bargains overheard across tables and
countertops
Capturing the imagination of an art dealer or an auctioneer

HAITI: BETTER FUTURE AHEAD

When the restavecs' dirty secret system ceases, a
reasonable and
descent but conscientious minimum wage establishes,
then real change as come

When natives no longer leave their beloved and cherished
homeland in droves
staked in commandeered unsafe boats and small vessels
Exploited, and purchased their boarding pass to sail for
the unwelcome and prestigious
Shores of America, the so-called promised land, then we
have arrived

When Haiti gets proper worldwide recognition and respect
fighting for
freedom and shading their crying blood of justice and
equality, then we have
obtained past due respect

When the so-called government and political leaders
embrace civilized
brothers joined in arms, accepted their differences, and
worked together for the
benefits of all the habitats and the entire country, then we
have overcome

When the burning tires are placed as a neckless around a
despised neighbor or a hate
political party opponent's neck be extinguishing, then we
have regained our humanity
and civility

When the Gourde, our national currency, no longer
bedeviled, minimized,
shunned, and demonized by the United States central
banks
When the imbalance and disparity are no longer five to
one ratio to the US
And the populous would accept their own currency rather
than carving and
Confiscating and hoarding the US mighty dollar
And our products and goods and exports are valuable,
sold, purchased, and on demand
Then we as a nation will be uplifted

TIGHT ROPE

Sneakers, black colored electrical lines,
sneakers hung high

Hung them high,
hung them lowg

Nikes, Pumas, my Adidas,
blow by blow

Converse, Filas, and New Balance,
checked out from life too soon

From rival gangs and illiteracy,
from the hypocrisy that densely justifies me

Burden added, sorrow multiplied,
another project housing or ghetto negative statistic
raises high

Rising from the ashes of despair,
cruel, brutal, no respect or appreciation for life

Not purchased by none, but claimed territory,
turf wars, homicides, and block parties are dumb

Having respect in the hood,

reputation to uphold at all costs,
the supremacy of life

Kamikazee pilots did not kill themselves,
but the enemy out there

So, don't hang them high, don't hang them low

DESPERATION OF DESPAIR

Our yellow butterflies are puny and fly lower
Not enough breeze or wind to make them fly high like the
mighty American eagle
High above the clouds and mountains possibly reaching
their full potential
Processes are given from above, that all butterflies are
created equal to be love and adore
Whiter green, blue, or monarch, noticeably seems by all
Is it the unprepared Cocom, or perhaps the hasty
caterpillar?
Or all lies, the lies and be trial that make them bitter
Little mind. Little faith, little blossom bodies

THE WHALING WALL

What is that whaling so famous and admired by all

Respected by many for its fulfillment of past prayed
sentiments

Niches carved in its Western façade hiding the faithful
prayers of all

Many come from far away for a lifetime pilgrimage joyful
journey

Not hearing, learning, and contemplating how to hate and
kill the East and the West

But for pure religious revenge, martyrdom, and Jihad of
what they stand for

Standing strong of a mixture of mortar, sweat, and blood;
bounding all mankind to one
likely purposed

Recognizing a higher power, request, petitions, and fate
and hope in the upcoming
future

OASIS OF LOVE TOO

43

Mountains of love,
breast peeking up like pyramids toward the sky

Palm branches swinging on the wing, as her dark shiny
hair provides some shade

Moist, juicy, and warmth,
is the feeling of the smooth but hard penetration?

She stands tall and firm as a palm Royal tree,
and like a palm tree in Lebanon

CRY LITTLE BOY CRY

Who will wipe away his desperate and sorrowful tears?
Cry little boy, cry
Who will take away his dark night fears?
Cry little boy, cry
Who will make things better?
Cry little booboo, cry
Who will stop the awful and bitter taste?
Cry little boy, cry
Who will say things will be better?
Cry little boy, cry

When the abuse continues at night,
Cry little boy, cry
When there is no way out, and he can't fight,
Cry little boy, cry
When he can't speak, and must keep it inside;
Cry little boy, cry
When no one will believe him or give him an ear,
Cry little boy, cry

Where can he go, for he is only five?
Cry little boy, cry
Where is the so-called place, where he can feel safe?
Cry little boy, cry
Where his embrace come from, or complete solace,
Cry little boy, cry

What was is crime or infraction
Cry little boy, cry
What did he do to deserve this punishment?
Cry little boy, cry

Why did someone see it coming?
Cry little boy, cry
Why did someone quickly interfere?
Cry little boy, cry
Why did God just strike them dead?
So, he can have complete peace in his head

FALSE IDENTITY

If I were God, I would not have created men,
For they are so foolish, so perverted, and so sinful

If I were a bird, I would fly over people's heads,
And drop droplets of feces all over their cheep's hats, old
wigs, and faded toupees

If I were a dog, I would go around and bite everyone who
did not give me a bone

If I were a mosquito, I would only fly in the big cities and
bite only the wealthy people
and infect the affluent with Zika and the West Nile viruses

If I were a woman, I would marry the richest man in the
world and divorce him for his money

If I were gay, my lovers would only be pretty, tall, and
athletic-looking young man

If I were a prostitute, I would infect every unfaithful man
with the HIV

If I were a banker, I would not let poor folks borrow
money to buy weeds and cracks

If I were white, I would live in the suburbs, attend private
universities, and retire at forty

If I were a judge, there would not be such thing as death
row; it would be a week row

If I were the sun, I would burn all those who do not use
sunscreen or sunglasses

If I were a baby, I would wet my diaper 50 times a day,
cry only at night,
and would drink five gallons of milk a day

If I were a professional athlete, I would be drug-free, stay
out of trouble, and don't
forget where I came from

If I were an ant, I would work destroying people's
manicured lawns and honeycake

If I were a cow, I would urinate in the milk that I produce
so that children can get sick

If I were a cop, I would shoot all the bad guys instantly,
and ascertain their innocence
after

If I were poor, I would have eleven kids and stay on
welfare forever

SELF-CONCEPT

When I look at myself,
I see someone good.
Not one without sin or blemish,
But one that can be understood

When I listen to myself,
I hear someone nice.
Not one with cold-blooded ice,
But one in which the feeling will last

When I smell myself,
I scent sweetness.
Not though the best,
But one which will not rest

When I taste myself,
I know I taste good.
Not a rotten yesterday's dish,
But some good fresh food

When I touch myself,
I feel warmth,
Not heat from a burning flame,
But overwhelming love from an overflowing heart

When I touch myself,

I feel the warmth coming from the earth's crust
Not negative or evil warmth,
But the real one straight from my heart

IN THE NAME OF NATURE

I am God who created you in my image
I am the sky who projects you from fallen aliens
I am the sun who warms the earth as it rotates on its axis
I am the clouds who give you a pillow as you fly over
I am the stars who lit your path shielding you from
spiking rocks
I am the wind who brings you the pleasant fresh garden
aroma
I am the tree who gives you a canopy for the midday sun
I am the dirt who grows your vegetation, dust to dust
I am the bird who starts your day with an angelic melody
I am the rain who washes your sorrows and worries away
I am the sea who guides your large naval bodies
I am the water that you drink to stay alive
I am the fish that you eat when you're tired of high-fat
red meat
I am the cow who produces milk for your morning cereals
I am the spirit who keeps you going day after day
I am the fruit who smoothens you're going day after day
I am the earthquake, flood, and tornado who eliminates
corrupt men
I am the moon who lightens your way as you stroll to
the park
I am the vegetable who provides fiber in your diet
I am the earth who provides you with energy
I am who I am

In the name of nature
I am who I am
I am nature

THANKSGIVING

Give thanks with a grateful heart
Give thanks to the Holy One
Give thanks because he has given, Jesus Christ his son

And now let the weak say I am strong
Let the poor say I'm rich
Because of what the Lord has done for us
And now let the sick say I'm whole, let the bound say I
am free
Because of what the Lord has done for us
Give thanks to the Lord with praises and thanksgiving

Thank you, God, for creating me in your likeness
Thank you, God, for loving me despite my weakness
Thank you for giving me your only son to die for all
my sins
Thank you for the Holy Spirit to guide me away from sins
Thank you for the gift of eternal life
Thank you for the precious breath of life
Thank you, God, for healing me and protecting me from
diseases
Thank you, God, for my parents and my family too
Thank you, God, for everything that I have
Thank you, God, for all your blessing
Thank you, God, for all your miracles
Thank you, God, for peace of mind
Thank you, God, for your word of truth

Thank you, God, for my education
Thank you, God, for my salvation
Thank you, God, for saving my soul

On this day of Thanksgiving, turkey, stuffing, and
trimming
I just want to thank you for the food on my table
Thank you for being there for me, and never forsaking me

WHAT IS LIFE?

Is life just the Big Bang or the evolution theory?
Is life indeed creation made in the image of its creator?

Is life just s clump of cells, a mass of bacteria, or a spec of
viruses?
Is it just ATP, mitochondria, DNA, RNA, and nuclei?

Is it just one day you are born, come to life, and die?
And the next you're old, frail, and can't even enjoy life

Is it just a passing fade, or is it to stay?
Is it just like the wind that we can feel and touch?

Is it purely materialistic processions, money, and wealth?
But when our eyes dim all things remain sadly behind

Life is fun, life is joy
Life is an underserving gift from the God-man above

Life is giving everything at any cost,
Yet, demanding nor expecting anything in return

Life is what you make out of it,
And not what you wish you had or could do with it

Life is short, changing, and unpredictable,
Life can also be fulfilling, stable, and pleasurable

Life is more than just work, bills, sadness, and sickness,
Life is about friends, family, success, determination, and stamina
Life is a gift, life is love, and life is everlasting

LONG LIVE YOUR MEMORY

Long live your memory
Forever I hope you live
I hardly knew you friend
I wanted to know you, cousin

You were full of life
You really loved life
Laughter erupted from your heart, and joy shined on
your face
Sorrow and regret reflect on mine

You loved the beauty of all shapes and forms
You love beauty whichever way it comes
Black, white Asians, you loved them all
I am proud to say that you were not the biggest

I know we don't always agree,
With a puppy in my bedroom, smoking, drinking, girls,
and fun
But that didn't mean that I was better than you
Because you lived a happy life without reservation

Before it was your mother that I didn't know
Now it's you that I wish I knew
I hope you see her again someday
Somewhere nice, peaceful, and joyful

My mother is devasted
She remembered and was not close to her
She never goes one year without seeing you
She's your aunt, I guess she's always be

I hope you made peace with your maker
Long live your memory
Forever, I hope you live

WHITE WATERS

Yes, this is the White House;
White rivers, lakes, and ponds around it
Look I'm a Clintonite
Why should I care?
After all, I'm the president
And a very good swimmer
So, what if I cheated
No one got hurt

It was a long time ago
And I was a jerk
The governor, I was
Debate is my reply
I didn't know
I was going to make it to the top
Becoming a president right on the spot

Yes, I'm the smart-ass layer
Five feet tall, slim like a ruler
Blond I'm, my mother recalls
Shut up you too, before I drop the booms
So, what if the health plans do not work
The entire cabinet is full of jerks

Yes, I'm Chelsey "Pretty Girl" Clinton you can see
All the boys know me from my town
You know what I mean

Don't drop your tongue
Virgin you taught me I was
I'm a sorry big ass
I go to private school, but I'm still a foul
Drugs and alcohol are all over the school

JESUS TWO

Jesus is the answer to the world today,
in a world full of confusion, turmoil, wars, and rumors of
wars,
I need Jesus.

Oh, how I love Jesus!
How can you love him who you do not see and not your
neighbor who you are?
You need Jesus.

Jesus is the way, the truth, and the life.
We must show the lost the way, tell the truth, and save
lives.
We need Jesus.

SHALOM

Shalom, Jerusalem,
Shalom, Israel

Peace be still.
And know that I am God
who forms the valleys and leaves on the hills?

Sabbath Shalom, Jerusalem
Sabbath Shalom, Israel

I am the God of your ancestors,
the God of Abraham, the God of Isaac, and the God of
Jacob.
March to the temples and synagogues to offer sacrifices of
praise and worship me.

Shalom Aleichem, Jerusalem.
Shalom Aleichem, Israel.

I have delivered you from the bondage of the Egyptians.
I have delivered you also from the Persians.
I have delivered you again from the Philistines.
I have sent you a Savior to deliver you from the Romains.
And I have sent you a Messiah to deliver you from sins.

THE BEAUTY OF A BLACK WOMAN

Twin perfectly well-rounded mountain peaks
surely kindly delicious ready to be adored.

Coarse black hair for Tarzan to swing from tree to tree.
Seductive eyes, clear like crystal with perfect vision.

Flatten rounded tip cool nose, able to detect a charlatan
from far.
Ears succulent for the enabler, sweeter than wild honey.

Tastes buds of the flavor of love spread and shadowing
her delicious tongue.
Her sparkling perfectly aligned teeth surely make the
ivory tusk of African craft envious.

SPIRITS OF MY ANCESTORS SET ME FREE

The spirits of our ancestors run deep and warm through my veins.
Reminding me of the pain and suffering long endured for it was not in vain.
"One day we shall surely succeed", proclaimed Mark Twain.
Formers ancestry slaves,
now finally ruling the free world.
We are strong and resilient.
As were our ancestors' silent and profound spirits.

MY EBONY

Black you are, thanks to the good God above.
Streams of thy strength flow through your veins.

Roots go deep into the earth.
Kindly ushering the birth of our offspring.

Princesses, queens of monarchy,
only you are my perfect ebony.

A strong will and skin texture
foremost resistant to the trials, getting ready for the
rapture.

SYMPHONY OF LOVE

Drumbeat rhythm of the season
like Beethoven's symphony of love.

Shakespeare's Broadway production of Romeo and Juliet,
south entry and exit into the portal of love.

Cadence balance to the six cords,
each note perfectly harmonized.

Do you or do you not want to know rhymes?
For the call and showers of love is soon to come

ROOTS

The blood of sorrow and pain of my ancestors cried from
within,
set me free and let me go!

To what I must reach to the higher deity,
to sore high, high like the Black angels of old.

Not fallen from disgrace,
but made in his image.

Lashes torn and imbedded our skins,
from the master's bloody dirty whip keep me tagged and
labeled.

Do this, do that, thinking I would not mine,
surely, I do, surely, I must go far.

To my bellowed land far away,
yes, back home to the dawn of a new day.

PHASES OF FLOWERS

Roses are red.
Violets are blue.
I hate you,
but you hate me too.
The divorce phase.

Roses are red.
Violets are blue.
I love you,
And you love me too.
Dating phase.

Roses are red.
Violets are blue.
I do not know what I must do,
and so, do you?
Honeymoon phase.

DANIEL SIMON PIERRE

THE MOST HATED MAN IN AMERICA

Who is this man full of pride and joy,
a tradesman and businessperson full of energy?

His only crime was to be born in opulence.
With a silver spoon in his mouth with a golden appearance

History was made when he came down
from the golden escalator inside the Trump Tower,
when he announced his historic presidential run
indeed to surely make things better for the USA.

His golden, shiny, sprayed hair,
attract and pull you in the snare.

His charisma and up-front spoken mind,
tells you like it is whether you like it or not.

It is the "New York" in him,
which flows warm like a flood.

A new wave and motto have come:
"Make America Great Again".

SENSES

Eyes, big angry eyes, looking at me,
as if looking for one to see.
Seducing glare of sensuality,
privately staring at me.

Dark distant sounds in the night pierce my peace
which I thought I should not dream of.
For a land far away,
that I dreamt of going all day.

Delicious aromas engage my taste buds,
to taste the sweetness of your embrace.
For it has been said,
the darker the berry, the sweeter the juice.

To feel you penetrate my core.
This immense peace forever.
Go far and far inside,
for there is even more real estate to explore.

Like a sweet aroma in the Garden of Eden,
your lovely fragrance overwhelms all my senses.
Aroma of roses, gardenias, and jasmines
forever looming from now to the end.

THE LOVE LANGUAGES

The time we cherish together
would be forever embedded in my mind.
My heart is overwhelmed by the quality
and not the quantity of time we spent together.

I want you; I need you, and you need you.
I cannot leave without as you only can do.
You are lovely, you are specular, you are magnificent.
Only you can understand my unspoken love accent.

You are an angel sent from above,
a perfect woman with no flaws which I adore.
You are wrapped in a bundle of love
sent via express mail from above.

My mind, my body, and my soul are for you,
to serve, please, and do what you want me to do.
A foot massage, a back rub, or internal penetration
for an internal orgasm without limitation.

I want to please you.
I want to touch you.
I want to please you.
And to do what only I can do.

IT HURT (MOLESTATION)

My angelic innocence was stolen one dreary raining dark
chilly night,
as I recall the horror and terror of what I felt
unwanted sexual advances required of me,
which I did not ask for or needed to be.

I was the prey in the domicile
for the hunter grasp grip, me from behind.
Not like a friendly familiar embrace from my beloved
siblings,
but from an older man which I was unwilling.

He took the parental vow to protect and do no harm,
so why he come to my room late that night and cause me
harm?
Mommy, where are you, where are you, are you sleeping?
Do you know and are you willing?

Closing your eyes to the unbearable truth,
that the man you wedded could be so untrue.
The illegal and unwanted touch
made me feel dirty and ugly,
losing my innocence far too early.

It did not happen only once from a night of drinking.
But repeated and felt its ugly head night after night in
worry.

No longer innocent, pure, or a virgin,
what would I tell my husband, or should I tell my story
from the beginning?

For the pain was, is, and will be each night the nightmare
began.
For it hurts so much and I want it to end.

THE COLD (AUSCHWITZ)

Back then, yes back, unprovoked, and unchallenged
in the cold, summer, or spring
packed like Kosher sardines to an unwanted destination.

The largest of the German Nazi concentration camps.
Over 1.1 million men, women, and children Jews were
exterminated.
The bright star of David lit no more,
dimed, dark, in unseen horror.

Our Holocaust of accusation and extermination
started with false claims, accusations, and Kristallnacht.
Everything taken away will be given to the predator.

But was it a secret, or all new but did not care?
They were only Gypsies and only unwanted Jews
which Hitler chose to eradicate and destroy?

He forgot his past and heritage.
His mother was a Jew, you know.

Train rides to no men land',
no boarding passes no return expected.
On the way to the gas chamber, you know.
The fastest way to see them go.

Bullets have become too expensive and take too long to
kill,
the war soon ending, let us hide the burning bodies,
horrors, atrocities, and cruelty.

Six million too many gone too soon,
striped of the dignity and cultural identity in this diary
cold dark night.

Invaded by the mighty Nazi's brutality.
Poland showed no resistance to this crisis.
Three different camps of no man-land.

Could we comprehend this disaster again?
The killing machine is on full display.
No room to grow or stay awake.
Two years of hell from 1940-1942,
finally closed in 1945 after the liberation from the Soviet
army.
1.1 million perished and died at Auschwitz.
Including one million Jews
sent to the gas chambers.
Or sentenced to forced labor
for repayment of the false accusation of
economical horror.

Sadly, the Nazi's killing machine at it is best,
As we were forced to pass the test.
Killing centers of concentration and labor camps

And the large gas chamber, smoke, cannot breathe,
suffocating and damp.

Families separated from birth breaking the bondage of
lineage.
For small, medium, and large families to fit and die.

Crematoria at Birkenau,
who is left to forget our rights and say no.
Mass murder camps and mass murder ramps
only contracted and constructed for European Jews.

WHO I AM?

To be or not to be that is the question.
To question or not to question that is to be.

What is to be?
What shall be the question?
What shall it be?
What shall be asked?
What shall it be?
What shall be answered?

Perhaps, nothing.
Perhaps, something.
Perhaps, no one.
Must be someone.

Who shall it be?
Who will find out?

Maybe you.
Maybe me.
You may see.

Who it shall be?

GOD

Who is God, who is He, who is She, who is it?
What is God, what is He, what is She, what is it?
When is God, when is He, when is She, when should it come?
Where is God, where is He, where is She, where would it be?
Why is God, why is He, why is She, why is it not to me?
How is God, how is He, how is She, and how it feels?

LOVE

Love is abstract, love is concreated.
Love is fogy, sometimes solid.

Solid and painful when I feel hurt,
whenever and each time you hurt my heart with pain.

Hurting so deeply that is felt in my marrow,
the deepest part of me where I grow.

Growing each day with undetermined length,
that is how long my love will stand.

MY ALPHABET

A is for apple
B is for boy
C is for cat
D is for dog
E is for elephant
F is for fun
G is for good
H is for hot
I is for imagine
K is kitty
L is for love
M is for mom
N is for not
O is for open
P is for purple
Q is for question
R is for respect
S is for sex
T is for top
U is for utilize
V is for victory
W is for water
X is for Xerox
Y is for yellow
Z is for zoo

COVETOUSNESS

Give me more, give me now.
Give me more, and give it to me now.

Give me more than I can keep.
Go ahead, I have room for it all.

Give me more than I can pay
for there is always a layaway.

Give it to me, make it fit, and make it feel good.
I want it, I like it, go ahead give it to me now.

OLYMPIAD

Athens, god Apollo, son Hercules
Brazil, braziers, capital of breast augmentations
Chicago, passing-smelling winds, presidential corruption
Atlanta, sad bumming, false accusation
Greece, swim like a fish, record eight gold medals
Montreal was clean and cold, the bill paid in 2009
Los Angeles, the Crips, and the Bloods,
sexy blond babes and the beach boys.
Moscow, Cold War, did not go through this boycott.
Madrid, good food, salsa music, and merengue.
Mexico City, siesta, don't drink the water,
and do not breathe polluted air.

HURRICANES

Sucks now only for a time
dynasty as an independent.
5 NCAA football championships,
Big East in your face, ass whooping with consistency
ACC same ass-kicking for all
Swagger, boasting, showboating
53 home games winning streaks
Many Heisman's winners
Most drafted players in the NFL,
wide right, right left in your face.
This is the "U" that I remember.

DEATH

Oh death, where is thy sting?
Oh death, where is thy victory?

Laugh now, but death cries later.

Oh death where is thy sting?
Oh death, where is thy victory?

Your sting may hurt me now,
but joy comes in the morning.

Oh death where is thy sting?
Oh death where is thy victory?

Victor, but not the victim no more.
Victory is mine in the name of Jesus.

THE FATHER

I'm the Father
Lord of all, and Lord for all
Father of all mankind, Father on your mind

My God, the God, your God, the only true God.
Most high, not low, but high above all and surely above
the clouds.
The everlasting God.

The Lord-will-provide
The Lord
The Lord God of heaven
Lord God
Beer Lahai Roi

WHAT'S HIS NAME

Savior
Lamb of God
Redeemer
Messiah
Jesus
Jesus Christ
Jesus the Christ
Bright of the morning star
Bread of life
Resurrection and life
Lion of the Tribe of Judah
Holly one
Alpha and Omega
The way, the truth, and the life
Immanuel
God with us
The child
A Nazarene
Lord
The Lord
Son of God
Lord our Lords
King of Kings
Teacher
Master
Son of man
Son of David

Son
John the Baptizer
Elijah, Jeremiah, the prophet
Son of the living God
Rabbi
I'm the God of Abraham, the God of Isaac, and the God
of Jacob
Jesus of Nazareth
King of the Jews
Son of the highest God
Carpenter
The son of Marie and brother of Joseph, James, Judas, and
Simon
Beloved son
Abba
Father
Son of the highest
Son of Joseph
Master of the Sabbath

HOLLY SPIRIT

Comforter
Holly Ghost
Holly Spirit
The one to come
God
Third person of the trinity
Fire
Wind

GOLF

Pot, three iron
Hole in one
Beardy that does not fly
Boggy bad play
Par and ego
Subpart like a submarine
Even par, even Steven
Ruff not smooth
Lake floating
Sinker in the sand

TENNIS

Net and rackets
John McEnroe arguing calls and smashing his rockets
Ace
Jimmy Connors's professionalism and class on the court
Deuce
Arthur Ashe first African-American grand slam winner
Breakpoint
Even Lindle European champ
Match point
Billy Jean King made history by beating a man
Fault
Chris Everett's sweetness and elegance in action
Judge
Martina Navratilova like the supernova
Line judge
The Williams's sister's pure brute force and big muscles
White lines and six ball boys.

HOCKEY

Wayne Gretzky the great French one,
Youngest rewrites record book, made history early.

Guy Lafleur french talented,
Skate like a swan with no helmet.

Gordy Orr is legendary,
A vanguard, trailblazer, historic.

Grand Fur, the black rubber pock doesn't pass him,
Guard the net like Fort Knox.

Ken Dryden protects the Madison Square Garden,
Another save, one more stop, another victory

Eric Lindros powerfully, but short leaves career,
city of love, love to skate and hit hard against the glass.

Mario Lemieux, French also, wears a helmet.
Stuck around, sickness retired too prematurely.

SEX

What is this immense feeling that is irresistible and
indescribable?
Orgasm to the max, stimulating all my senses, and quite
unbelievable

Climatic moment, hot erotic passion.
Seconds at most, but long-lasting hot memories and
emotions.

More mental than physical, you know.
Man thinks of me every six seconds they say.

Women don't get enough of me I know.
But I can also be obtained for a small fee that is.

FOOTBALL

Summer, humid, hot, drops of sweats
Winter, cold, freezing, blizzards
Raining, muddy, sleeper
Helmets, clits, and pads
Stadium, coliseum, white lines, man in black stripes
Captains at midfield, shake hands, coin toss, head or tail
Whistle blows, kick-off, and game on the way
Punting team, receiving team, and special team
First down, second down, third down, and fourth down
Yardage, move the oval leather pig skin
Offense and defense adjust, a couple of sacks, fourth
down, punt again
Another team, punt return, good blockage, crosses the
goal line
Touch down, six points, one extra point, the crowd goes
wild.

BASKETBALL

Bill Russell, 11 rings, old great timer
Wilt Chamberlain, once scored 100 points, dominating the paint
Julius Irving, "Doctor J", dunks from the top
Kareem Abdul Jabbar, skyhook unstoppable
Larry Bird, unpassable shooting
Irving "Magic" Johnson, no look pass, plays all positions
Dominic Wilkins, dunking champion and MVP
Darrel Dunken, pure power, broke baskets many times
Shaquille "Shaq" O'Neal, broke basket too, rapper and comedian
Kobe Bryan, once scored 81, gone too soon
Dewayne Wade, unstoppable in the paint
LeBron "King "James, the best player in the NBA, but not a champion yet
Michael "Air "Jordan, 3 dunking titles, 6 times finals
MVP, 6 championships,
9 scoring titles, 2 Olympic gold medals,
4 times league MVP, no look free throw,
spectacular moves by Michael Jordan exclaimed Marv Albert

BASEBALL

Empire
First base Empire
Second base Empire
Third base Empire

First base
Second base
Third base
Home plate

Single play
Double play
Triple pay

Single
Double
Triple
Home run

Strike one
Stick two
Stick three
You're out

Ball one
Ball two
Ball three

Walked

One run
Two runs
Three runs
Grand slam

GOD TWO

God is the one that created you,
according to his image, according to his likeness.

God is good all the time, and all the time God is surely
good,
even though you may not understand his purpose for you.

Things may even never seem to go your way,
God is still all-knowing, all-seeing, and all-powerful

God is infinite and everlasting,
although you can't begin to comprehend its beginning
or end.

God is the one that makes the Earth rotate around the sun,
and provide its warmth while growing its vegetation.

God makes the stars and moon fit harmoniously in the
firmament,
that provides illumination after the sun says goodnight.

God is God all by himself and does not need anyone's
help,
does not need to be defined, explained, boxed in, and
scientifically theorized.

JESUS

Jesus is the answer to the world today,
in a world full of confusion, turmoil, wars, and rumors of
wars,
I need Jesus.

Oh, how I love Jesus.
How can you love him and not your neighbor?
You need Jesus.

Jesus is the way, the truth, and the life.
We must show the way, tell the truth, and save lives.
We need Jesus.

HOLLY GHOST

Holly Ghost comes into this place
Feels me and makes me whole
As whole as I can be
To continue my journey
On this earth, in this world

FOOD

Cold food
Hot food
Spicy food

Liquid food
Solid food
Junk food

Palatable
Tasty
Nasty

American
Canadian
European

Taste bugs
Delicious
Gordon blue

FAMILY

Abraham, Isaac, and Jacob
Nucleus, extended and blended
Mother, father, children
Diapers, bottles, and wipers
Fights, fits, and near miss
Love you, hate you, and can't do without you
Calls 911, runs away, and DCF
Need you, don't care, won't swear

HERE I AM

Here I am Lord, use me
Make me, shape me, and mold me
Send me and I will go
Charge me and I will grow
Grow to show the world
How much you love them
That you sent your only son
To die for me in my place
A place of desolation, agony, shame
For indeed you remember my name
Long ago written in the Lamb book of life
With your indelible blood that was shed on the cross
Open is the first book then the second book
Whose names not found written
Will not enter the promised land.

POLITICS

Politics is a dirty game,
if you don't have the stomach for it, don't play the game.

Republicans, Democrats, Independents

Politics is hot and steamy,
if you can't stand the heat, get out of the kitchen.

Conservatives, Liberals, undecided

Politic is nasty,
if you want to stay clean, don't take illegal kickbacks.

Right, left, and center

Executive branch,
white house, Oval Office, 1600 Pennsylvania Avenue, I
did not have sex with that woman, community organizer,
or Illinois junior senator, just speeches, just words.

Acorn, register, vote often

Legislative Branch,
bills, the president signed or vetoed, and laws passed.

Majority, sixty percent, philoboster

Judicial Branch,
District court, circuit court, appellate court, Supreme
Court.

Liberal, conservative, constitutional judges.

Senators,
town meetings, poles, votes to benefit constituents; do for
me first, awesome,
well-spoken, good speeches.

Do as I say, immorality, caught with pants down

Congressmen,
enact laws for others to follow but not for them.

Don't watch me, follow the law, don't you get it

Vice president,
Presides over the House, tie bracer, in the shadow, wish he
was the president.

Councilmen, commissioners, mayors,
Small timers, insignificant.

Governors,
most to become presidents, term limit, and Watergate.

THE BLOOD

Oh, the blood of Jesus,
it will never lose its power.
The power to love,
The power to forgive
The power to save,
The power to make amend.

It flows deep, down, and warm,
Like the river Nile
Grasping along in its path,
All that was not right
To make them righteous,
To make them all right

Like the stars in the sky,
That shines bright at night
To illuminate our path to him,
And save us from within
From Adam to Eve,
Needed desperately to cleave

USA ONE

Unity, united, unique
Safety, security, satisfaction
Harmony, ambition, acquire

Land of the free and home of the brave

What other country on earth,
That an alien can come on shore with nothing,
But have so much

Land of the free and home of the brave

Accomplish the dreams of their forefathers,
I Dreamt so long ago,
That could only be seen clearly here
Land of the free and home of the brave

Dreams to make in the Big Apple,
And eat the biggest slice of pie

Land of the free and homes of the brave

Work hard, save money, invest, and go to school
Married, two children, buy a car, home and picket fence

OH CANADA, HEY!

O Canada, how cold thy art,
Thy winter harsh,
White snowflakes fall
Subzero temperatures freezing the artic bands
Close to the North Pole
See the polar bears roll

O Canada, how too clean thy art,
Sweeps thy streets daily
As thy moon sleep
Trash picked up often
No illegal dumping allowed
Big fines to follow

O Canada, how warm thy art,
New green grass sprouts from thy ground
Butterflies dance in thy full leaf's trees abound
Serving as a canopy for thy buzzing honeybees
Temperate climate, smooth summer braze
Feeling like paradise only thy can bring

O Canada, how cool thy art,
Dry cool day
Long windy night
Snippy, nippy, runny nosy
Windbreaker, sweater, and scarfs
To protect from thy windy nights

O Canada, how live thy art,
New buds on branches limbs
Revived thy sleeping things
Hibernating grizzly bears awaken
Smelling the aroma of the honey bees
Come out of the cave to paw the nest

O Canada, how live thy art,
New buds on branches limbs
Revived thy sleeping things

THE CROSS

That ragged, bloody, old wooded stick,
So despised and rejected
Not appreciated and accepted by all,
But stained and bleed for all
For all humanity that seeks peace,
For their souls and lives
Eternal life is only obtained from the Son,
The real Jesus who died for all or only one
Its sight repulses me,
Yet, its shadow protects me
Preserving me from going to hell,
Where unbelief would make my soul fail
Fallen so far away from me,
Where I can no longer be seen
Seen for truly who I am,
A sinner found guilty by the law

HAITI

What have you done since 1804?
Freedom came at a greater cost for more
Cutting heads and burning houses
Wasted resources and forces
Long ago, once ago named Pearled of the Antilles
Larger, prosperous, abundant and flowering united
Hispaniola
Smaller, embargo, and poorest in the Western Hemisphere
divided, Haiti
Haiti travesty or tragedy
The US and UN had their say
Nothing but failures all the way
Permeated through the ages even to this day
Gruesome cruelty and abuses of civil rights
Lawlessness and surely no human's rights
Acid splashed to faces disfiguring, burning tires to necks
Serving as fashion necklaces
It is who you know, not what you know
An uncle and an aunt can only help
Abuses, discriminations, class biases, and unfairness
Lawlessness, lack of regulations, and oversights
No minimum wages, having Restavegs, surely slavery in
the 21st Century
Labady for tourists only, locals can't enter or afford it
Anarchy, tyranny, falsity, that's my Haiti

ISRAEL

Land of our Jewish forefathers; Abraham, Isaac, and
Jacob
Land that we will own and possess forever, our promised
land
For our sweets, shed blood, broken bones, and dead
bodies
Paved the way for our repossession in 1947 and
recognition in 1948
Promises by the only true God over two thousand
years ago
Zion nation growing by leaps and bounds, and the Zionist
movement is strong
From the Red Sea to Egypt, from Syria to Lebanon
The pomegranate provides sweet juice to crunch our taste,
The tall majestic olive trees provide extra virgin olive oil
to light our lamps and
and our Menorah
From the Knesset to the Sanhedrin our holiness remains
From the blowing of the Shofar to the proclaimed start of
the Sabbath,
to the Wailing Wall Wall bowing down and reading the
Torah
Wrap with the prayer shawl praying for peace thus far
Our resolve and determination to survive is stronger than
that of our enemies
We will fight till the end until the entire Muslim and
Islamic world understand

From Jerusalem to Bethlehem the city of David,
From the West Bank to Palestine
From Tel Aviv-Yafo to Haifa, to the Dead Sea
To the Sea of Galilee, to Eilat, and Tel Aviv
The Star of David shines even brighter
From the Golan Heights to the dissolved settlements
The promised land is ours, will not give up the West Bank
and East Jerusalem

EMMANUEL

Who is this child wrapped in swaddling clothes?
Laid in a manger, no room in the inn

All hotels and motels were closed
No palace to lay his head

Forced to be borne in an animal trough
The manager was rough

This holy child was born in humility,
To save humanity from its pity

Setting the example paving the way
To save our lives from an impending heel of doom

I KNOW WHY THE BIRDCAGE DOES NOT FLY

No transferable foundations, corporations, businesses,
wills, or trusts
Poverty rampant minds and heart bursting pain, anger, and
mistrust

White men died leaving behind a will
Black men get killed and leave behind bills

Growing far apart
Terrible cost of success thus far

Broken winds, unfulfilled dreams
Hopeless, lack of aspirations, devotions, or visions

Absent fathers, abusive stepdads, teenage mothers, babies
having babies
Houses in shambles, projects rambles

No hugs, support, reading a book, and a good night kiss
Need pride, self-esteem, and promises

Lack of formal education and graduation
Full mortuaries overcrowding penal institutions

Formaldehyde substitution for education
Guns blazing degrees burnings

No high school diploma, GED, or certificates
Sadly, no technical skills, associates, and surely no
bachelorette

No master's degrees, master of minds doing hard time
Surely no hope for a Ph. D. for you maybe, but not for me

Single mothers, parents, struggling alone,
To raise themselves, what was not foretold?

ANGELS

Angels in the sky, angels in disguise
Please watch over my soul when I die
Taken on your winds to a better world, which I don't
yet know
Never been there before, but surely I must go
Hope to see all that I've heard while lingering in this
black stretch hearse
Shining brass, trumpets blowing, waking up the sleeping
beauties
Place of peace, destined for a good sleep
No more sorrows or tears to be shed
Only good night's sleep, when I lay my head
On soft blue fluffy clouds of joy
Singing, hallelujah like Leroy
One that didn't succumb to temptations
While residing in his temporary situation
Where cancer, pain, and diseases ravage his body
But through it all remain holly
Not perfect by any stretch of the imagination
But only did his very best in most situations
As the pearly gates open wide to let him in
To see St. Peter's and St. Paul standing
With one holding the key to the pearly gates
And the other holding the open book that contains
my name

YOU ARE THE FUTURE, THE FUTURE IS YOU

If not you, then who?
If not now, then when?
If not here, then where?
If not that, then what?
If not for, then why?
If not, then how?

Come on, rightly claim your spotlight
For you are the future and the stars shine bright

Shining through the darkness of despair
That leaves one or two without any air

Breathing becomes impossible and unbearable,
Must hope and dream of what appears might seem
impossible

Probability and no sure certainty
Nothing is easy or given for free

You must work, and you shall work hard for it
You would appreciate it

So don't blame others and don't be negative
But accept personnel responsibility and the reality

So don't point fingers and learn to forgive and forget

Through that, you shall truly achieve, be healed, and
persevere

The dream has not vanished or faded away in the night
For it is your personnel manly duty to make it right

So march silently and patiently, and speak softly
Be very smart and live freely

Fly high, think big,
Reach to the sky and make your bid

Of who would do well or succeed,
Of who would be deceased and buried

To the next venture that is on the horizon
Don't lose your hope and all your vision

For we count on you and hope in you,
For you are the future,
And the future is you.

THE THRONE

Where was God when some of the Islamic and Muslim
radicals were zealots?
Plotted, conspired, and schemed to economically
overthrow the US
Seating on the throne!

Where was God when the two hijacked planes?
Flew high like eagles hitting the two Twin Towers in NY
at full speed,
And instantly becoming two large blazing furnaces of
blazed and despair
Seating on the throne!

Where was God when the innocent 3,000 victims became
collateral damage?
Some burned in throbbing anguish; skin pealing and
falling, undistinguished,
Others jumped to their end and others frantically ran
Some ran in flight, and some froze in fright
Others wondered what they did, and others were suddenly
and horribly deceived
Seating on the throne!

Where was God when over three thousand souls from the
world?
All dies in a twinkling of an eye, back on September
11, 2001

And instantly meeting their maker at once, on the other
side of town
Seating on the throne!

Where was God when? Still sitting on the throne!

WORSHIP

I worship you, oh mighty God, there is none like you
Who can substitute for God, who can take his place and
not sob?

I worship you, oh prince of peace that is what I want to do
Who can do what God does, his mighty hands outstretches
all

I give you praise, for you are my righteousness
Rightness is God, our only God,
And the Lord, our only Lord

I worship you, oh prince of peace, there is none like you
You are my God and my all, my hope, my dream, and all
that I hope for

For you alone belongs the glory, for you alone belongs the
praise
Hallelujah to the highest, praise be to our God, who seats
on the throne and
Who reigns forever, and forever, and forevermore?

Father we love and adore you, father we want to see
your face
Cherubims and seraphim and archangel bow down and
worship you
Saying holy, holy, and holy is the Lord, our God.

The Shema,
"Hear, O Israel: The Lord our God is one Lord. The
Shema".

SHALOM

Shalom, Jerusalem
Shalom, Israel

Let he who fears the Lord of peace praise him
Shalom, Israel

From Abram to Sarai, and from Abraham to Sarah
Shalom, Israel

Let the 12 tribes of Israel overtake and dominate the
promised land
Shalom, Israel

With outstretched hands and dry feet, stand still and see
the power of our lord
Peace be still and know that I'm still your God who
delivered you from oppression

AFTERWORD

Hello again, my dearest, faithful readers, and followers! Thanks to BooxAI and the great professional supporting collaborative team, I have other upcoming books and will continue to write and encourage the public until I run out of ideas.

After writing a series of poetry books (10 or 15) my goals, if the good Lord permits, are to write a cooking book (December), an exercise book (January), secular novels, and Christian motivation books in the near future, Sunday school lessons books, sermon book, and a prayer book. But in the meantime, please enjoy my first three submissions:

Book of Poetry (I Shall Rise)
Words from Above (Inspired)
Poetry of Love (I Love You)

Respectfully yours,

Dr. Daniel Simon Pierre
Writer / Poet
"The French Collection"